Dear Shaquan,

First let me start I know it has been a goal of yours for quite some time now. And it's good to see it finally happening for you. The trials you have gone through; the obstacles you've faced; the opposition you've conquered; the fears you've faced; the friends you've lost and the scars you've gained throughout this journey have somehow formed into these writings.

I remember when you first started writing. I remember the day you were in Ms. Harris first grade class and you snapped on Aaron Hall, who was one of your classmates at the time, who by the way you later grew to be really good friends with. But the outcome of that situation was counseling. You had to go to see Ms. G who was the school counselor at that time, with your mom and your aunt Ronda. In that session you were mute. You starred off into space and said not one word. You wouldn't talk to Ms. G, you wouldn't even look at your mom, and you said nothing to Ronda at all. But you were listening. Your ears were open enough for you to hear everything being said. You heard them talk about the possibility of there being abuse at home. You listened to the ignorance of the counselor implying that maybe you were neglected by your mother. You listened to your mom say that you were normally not a violent child. You watched the tears fall from her eyes as she began to think of herself as unfit. You watched Ronda stare off into space just not believing what she was hearing. And it all stuck with you. Especially the last thing you remember hearing that day.

After you got home, your mom sat you down and talked to you. She called your father and told him she don't know what to do. She was desperate and reaching out to anyone she could think of. Finally she told you a story of something she learned to do as a child after an unfortunate incident with one of her mother's friends. She told you how she learned to write. She explained how she didn't feel that she was understood. She talked about how no matter how much she talked to her mom, no one would believe her. But she said she wrote. She got some paper and wrote down everything she wanted to say. Knowing that if no one else understood, or if no one else heard it, it would benefit her to get it out and not hold it in. She explained to you how holding things is probably the reason you snapped that day. You were fed up within yourself, and you had no outlet, so you exploded internally. I remember watching you cry as she talked to you. This was the longest conversation you had ever had with your mom. This was the first time she vented to you. Sharing the deep thing within herself that she fought for so long to hide and bury. But she shared them with you… In an attempt to get you to try to write your feelings since you felt you couldn't talk to anyone.

From that moment on, you've been writing every sense. What started as a journal grew into a diary. Then from a diary it evolved into poetry. I remember you entering and winning poetry competitions in school and having your writings entered into local competitions and having your writings printed in the Star Ledger newspaper. I watched as that sheltered boy became more social. I watched as you went from being this isolated and disclosed child into one of the most popular kids in school. I watched as you went from being bullied and picked on, to having other kids volunteer to fight for you. I saw you began to take up for the other kids who were being bullied. Until the point where you were not just recognized by the student body, but amongst the faculty and staff you were known. You were utilized in speaking engagements. You were volunteered for public speaking and creative writing classes. You were voted to do all the end of year speeches. You became the writer you are today.

One of the most vivid memories I have of you, was when you wrote something spiritual for the first time ever. You wrote something for your grandfather's funeral. You stood up for the first time in front of a body of people you never saw, and you read it. You shook, you rocked, you stuttered, you cried, and you slobbered .... But you got through it. And when you finished you felt as if the poem you had just read somehow freed the spirit of your grandfather. You marvel at the reaction of the church you stood in. You felt something come over you that you had never felt before in writing nor in performing.

It was from that moment that you made up in your mind that your writing was now more than just a way to express yourself, but a gift. This writing thing was a gift that had to be shared. That somehow, this "gift", was tied to your purpose in life. You felt that this God, whom you only knew of and heard about before that moment, actually knew you. That in fact, he had a plan for your life that in some way included you writing. You went back home after that funeral in North Carolina, and you tried to wrote poetry as you always have, but you couldn't. It was as if once you were exposed to your writing purpose you were unable to return to just writing for fun.

It was not long after that, that you took your journey from New Jersey to North Carolina. You sought for that feeling you had in that church. You returned to that church and you sat and listened for the first time ever to preaching. You opened a bible for the first time in your life and read it for yourself. The pastor if that church, who later became your mentor, spoke words of destiny in your life. He told you that you had ministry in you. He told you there was a calling on your life. All of which was just Japanese to you at the time, but you listened. And those words never left your spirit. That pastor took you under his wing, and he taught you the scriptures. He spent hours upon hours a day to feed you the word of God. He took you on the road with him, and invited you into his home. That man became your spiritual father. He became your mentor, a father figure, a friend, a teacher and a role model to you. That man was Apostle John A. Bennett. The man you follow unto this day.

Shaquan, as a son, a friend, a brother, an adjutant, a servant and as a man… you have grown and unselfishly so. You reach back to anyone who straggles. You push anyone slowing down. You have motivated, encouraged, pushed, pulled, fought for, assisted, challenged and befriended everyone you could along the way. Yes you were stubborn, hard headed at times, bad, rude, rebellious, and even ran from God, but it was all part of the process to get you to where God has called you to be.

I pray that this be the first of many books for you. I pray your understanding and knowledge of the word saves, sets free, and delivers every person that reads your books. I pray the hands of God continue to cover you throughout your journey.

God Bless You

Faith Without Works

After the death of Christ the apostles went on a journey get the world saved. They wanted to reach everyone that they came across. Throughout the bible we see accounts of the many marvelous works that they did in every town they went to. The souls they came across weren't even thinking about a Christ or salvation but they got saved. They walked up and down the world converting souls to Christianity. Twelve men turned the world upside down!! Twelve men!!

During the "great conversion" of the world by the apostles, they took upon them seven deacons. They took seven men to assist them in their journey to convert the nation. And the bible says that they did just that. While the apostles where on their face praying and seeking counsel from God, and while they were not to be disturbed from this, the deacons handled things until it was time to lay hands and anoint people.

Quan's Corner:

Every week, Christians attend their church services in their local assembly. Pastors, and Bishops, Apostles, Prophets and Mega Apostles, or whatever else they want to call themselves, boast about their membership, their gifting and their callings. And the members attend faithfully, getting refilled weekly with their "dose of the holy ghost". And since we know the story, and are aware of what Christ has done, our faith today is on the level that it is.

That's all fine and well. Lord knows we all need that tune up, oil change, or word of encouragement to keep us on track. But what isn't fine is what the church has become. People talk about how much their "church be jumpin", and how, "we had church!!"... But I don't really think we know what church is anymore.

The apostles, the deacons and followers of Christ all had church. Church is when souls are revived. Church is where SINNERS are saved. Church is when people, who weren't saved before are saved. Souls are baptized! People are filled with the Holy Ghost. Church is when the blind see, the deaf hear, and the lame walk. Church is when shackles are broken, burdens are lifted, relationships are renewed long term and not just until next service. Church is when the presence of the Lord is evident, and the Power of the Lord liberates, and dominates...

But that's another page, let me stay on track.

Today church has become a ritual. People go to church now just because grandma went and they taught us to go. People go to church today just because it's what they are used to doing. They've done it every Sunday or Saturday, which ever your Sabbath, and so they continue to do it.

Well, brother author, how can you say that? Well look at the facts, if 12 men can turn the world upside down, and seven men can convert a nation... then why can't a church with a membership of 100 or more convert their little city or town. How can a church with 400 members not be able to win Chicago, or Raleigh. Why can't the combination of 25 churches, having 100 members a piece not win the state of North Carolina or North Dakota? Those are the facts. There are more people out here hungry for the word, hungry for Christ, longing for a relationship more so now than ever. People don't understand what's going on in their lives and they want answers. We know the church is the answer. We know Christ is the answer and the missing link to every void. Give it to them...

This may get too long so I’m gone cut it off here, but I believe I've express this thought fully. Saints and friends we have a lot of work to do. How many of us can fully say we do ALL we know to do in Christ to enhance the kingdom of God? I don't think any of us can say this honestly, including me. Know ye not that we will be judged according to the very works we do and the lack thereof as well? Let’s get busy y’all. The harvest is plenty but the laborers are few.

I pray I have said something to spark a fire under someone. I pray I’ve said something to push them to press towards the mark of the prize of the high calling in Jesus Christ. I know I cannot do it. I am almost certain that you can’t do it. But I believe with everything in me, that we can do it together, with the spirit of God dwelling in us, all things are possible.

May the Lord god continue to keep and cover you all until He meets us in the air. God Bless

Can You Hang

CYH while they talk about you to everybody they know and to some folks they don't?
While they lie on you and attempt to run your name through the mud, some wont
CYH while they belittle you, mudsling, gossip, meet about you and back bite?
When those whom you thought were for you, stood on the same side as those that were against you when it came time to fight
CYH when those whom you called friend used, abused, connived and plotted against you?

When you are forced to smile, while inside you mad as hell because they doing you dirty and without recompense… You…
Follow the word of God, and bless those that despitefully use you.
And you have to fast, supplicate, intercede and pray in faith for those who cursed you
CYH when you put in a situation where no one believes you and you can't prove your innocence?
When even family becomes foe and have taken side with the opposition and nonsense?
CYH when you read the Word of God and it says something like vengeance is His and for you to hold your peace?
When you could really destroy your accusers if you wanted to, and would be justified in doing so, in your mind at least?
CYH when you are in a position where you have to forgive no matter what they've done, only so you can continue to be forgiven?
And you have to love them and feed them and clothe them no matter how foul they livin
CYH when you have to apologize and make peace even when you were in the right?
When you are forced to stand alone after being forsaken by those who stood with you, them that you took up for in their fight
CYH when your flesh is on fire and that person that's not your spouse, does everything except put it in for you?
When you're stressed from the trials of life and the opportunity to drink or smoke come and you have to decide that's not what you're going to do
CYH when you have to keep changing friends and cutting off family members because they are not going where you're going? And have to just say good-bye
Or when you don't fit in. Feeling like you're not fit to live but not ready to die?

Can You Hang???

Quan's Corner

Well, we all have to think about these things. We are all put in these situations daily as Christians, and as people period. It burdens me to hear unsaved people talk about how hard they got it, when they robbin', stealin', lyin', killin', smokin', sexin', drinkin', plottin', switchin', bangin'... and whatever else they want to; While we are required to live a life of righteousness. Resisting temptation, overcoming evil with good, traveling the road less traveled, and believing that "change is gonna come", no matter how it looks and by no power of our own. Truth is life is easy when you know that if you don't get paid next week you will just go steal it from someone else. It's not hard to walk with your head held high knowing that when your accusers come, you'll just shoot them. What will they do when you can't? What will they do when the outcome of victory is not in their hand, but solely predicated upon someone else's speed, timing, methods and level of tolerance? Who really got it harder? Who really tougher? Who the real "G"? Can they really hang?

Brothers and sisters I know a man that aint just talk about it. I know a man who did it, and until this day will still do it for you. He hung and He didn't have to! He could've come down. He could've complained. He could've changed His mind. If ANYBODY was ever justified in doing so, it was Him, simply because He saw you. He saw what you did and what you were going to do. Truth be told, you don't deserve this type of grace for your actions, but He hung anyway. He was cursed so that you can be blessed. Yet and still, you go around doing thing to curse yourself even after he died so that you wouldn't be. He was imprisoned so that you can be free. Yet you still do things to be jailed, incarcerated, and bound by the sinister thoughts of your own mind. He became ordinary so that you could be extraordinary. He put down immortality and put on mortality. He died that you might have life. Yet you kill off yourselves and each other with the man-made poisons daily. He bled so that you might be in perfect health. He was beaten so you can have perfect peace. He saw what you did, heard what you said, (sometimes even about him), knew that you would give into the enemy's ways, but He hung anyway!!

That man is Jesus!! Our Lord and Savior Jesus Christ the Righteous.

So if you haven't already taken the time to thank the man that did hang, because you weren't tough enough to, then you ought to take a moment right now to do so.

Give it up for the real "G"!! God All Mighty!!

Betrayal Of A Brother

"Yea, mine own familiar friend, in whom I trusted, which did eat of my bread, hath lifted up his heels against me." - Psalms 41:9

"... for a man's enemies are the men of his own house." - Micah 7:6

"They have prepared a net for my steps; my soul is bowed down: They have digged a pit before me, into the midst thereof they have fallen themselves. Se'lah." - Psalms 57:6

These and many more are quotes from the bible, that tells us what is now a widely known epic that has frustrates the minds and hearts of millions of people around the world even until this day. Even back in the bible days, people being screwed, manipulated, put down, slandered, sold out, and even sometimes killed by their own friends and family has baffled the minds of mankind. It's sad that here we are nineteen hundred and sixteen years later we still have the same problem.

In the bible there were countless examples of this. In fact, I'll share some of them with you now. Moses was abandoned by his parents and placed in a basket in the Nile River. Elisha was scorned by the other prophets in Elijah's school. Joseph was sold into slavery by his brothers. Abel was killed by his brother Cain. James and John couldn't get along. David's son raped his own sister. Reuben slept with his father's concubine. Laban tricked Jacob into marrying Leah instead of Rachel. Esau sought to kill Jacob. Lot conspired against Abraham. Abraham pimped his wife. Delilah tricked Sampson into telling her his weakness only to deliver him into the hands of the Philistines. Peter denied Jesus. Not to mention the greatest of all... Judas sold out Jesus for a few dollars. All through the bible we see betrayal. We see envy leading to conspiracy. We see just some messed up stuff. Most of which was carried out by the hands of near kinsmen.

Quan's Corner:

Too many times today we come across phony persons; people that appear to be with you. They go through all the trouble and all the motions of presenting themselves as a friend. They come around often. They speak good verbiage. They earn themselves a good name amongst those you are closest to. They laugh and joke with you. They eat with you. They stand *beside* (not with) you for all those to see. Some even go as far as to even fight beside you. On your side, like they got your back and best interest at heart.

Only to find later, that you have been befriended only to be betrayed; To be talked about; To be slandered; To be conspired against; To be lead into a trap of emotional ambush. All the while, all the time they spent gaining your trust, was just a plan to get you to lower your guard; to let down your wall; to disarm your spiritual security system and retract all defenses. Ultimately, leaving you vulnerable, and in a state of defenselessness; placing you in a state where you can easily be overtaken. They were indeed, "your friend til the end", just like Chucky.

That's the wonderful thing about being found in the will of God. It demands heaven's backing. And when we fail to be obedient enough to set our affections on things above, when the love we develop for someone, begins to cover a multitude of their sins; When our feelings begin to serve as a veil, blocking us from what is, revealing only what appears to be; The Lord is gracious enough to protect us, and those "friends", don't realize that the only thing they have done, is put you in a position to rule over them. How is that Brother Author? The moment they conspire against you, they automatically make themselves lower than you. Prove it Quan! They go from being friends to enemies, our footstools. He said that when they come to eat of our flesh, they will ALL stumble and fall. He has already given us the victory over all of our enemies. He promises not to let any harm come near us. And He is constantly protecting us from dangers BOTH seen and unseen. That's why, no matter what people do, or where they come from, we as Christians, have to learn to keep our motives pure. So we are careful to be found in the will of God. The moment we conspire, or our motives are no longer pure, we lose that backup protection plan, and we then make ourselves an enemy to the other person.

Brothers and Sisters, continue to pray. Pray that the Lord keeps us in a position to remain humble. Pray that He helps us to utilize our spiritual scissors. Pray that He keeps us ready to cut the ties that bind us to people who only seek to destroy us or those who don't add to our lives, that way, we will have less emotional scars. Friends are only an issue while they are still friends, because we place them in that "inner circle". But the moment they conspire and make themselves an adversary or an enemy, IMMEDIATELY, God grants us victory over the attack of every enemy set against us.

Until next time brothers and sisters, saints, friends and foes; May the Lord God bless you real good. I pray I said something to help you out. If not, I pray I put something on your mind.

Stay true. Stay encouraged. Stay focused. Stay in His will.

God Bless

Don’t choke on the seed

(cultivating seeds)

Everything that God created He called good. He assigned a purpose to everything. And to every purpose assigned He, commissioned an opposition, in an attempt to equip the mind of man to work as an overcomer.

One of the most fascinating creations God made, at least in my opinion, is one of the world's lowest life forms. It holds one of the most overlooked and under minded purposes in all of creation. Yet without it, life would probably not be functional at all. I’m talking about dirt/soil.

The messed up thing is that soil never gets to decide which seeds get placed in its care. And never has the choice to accept or reject seeds. If it’s the right time of year, it just matures that seed. Without question, without bias, without hesitation, it nurtures every seed the same way.

The dirt protects the seed from the fowl of the air. It regulates the temperature of the seed for proper cultivation. And no matter how many storms pass, it holds on to the seed and protects it until it is mature enough to protect itself. And the outcome of its efforts, aren't just flowers. It is the smile on the face of a wife on Valentine's Day; the wages of a florist used to take care of her family; the peace of mind of a spouse in the garden of the home; the home of some squirrel or fowl or chimp; the source of food for herbivores that feed the meat we feed on; it is the oxygen in every breath we take each passing second of everyday. And so forth and so on... you see its significance.

Quan's Corner:

Spiritually, the dirt we know here on earth is known in the heavenly as the heart. I've always been told, and now have come to believe, that soil in the spiritual realm represents the heart here in the natural realm. And in life there are planters everywhere. And although nobody's growing tulips in their bodies, we are all nurturing seeds of some sort planted by people. Some of which we know and other we are not aware of. These are seeds of fear, doubt, depression, sorrow, faith, hope, peace, and many more different types of seeds randomly and often times subconsciously, that we nurture on a daily basis.

Difference is, unlike dirt, we have the choice to accept or reject and pluck out the seeds we don't want to cultivate. Whether by way of television, radio, media, or mouth through conversation, we have the choice to either hold them or to pluck them out. We don't have to dwell on, entertain, or play with the ideas of things others attempted to put in us.

Every conversation, every show we watch on tv, every hour we listen to Tom Joyner, Russ Par, Michael Basin, even Yolanda Adams, or Michael Reese for that matter, these are all seeds attempting to find a place in the garden of our hearts to be cultivated. And it's not always easy to pluck them out after they are planted, because much like the dirt, the heart will protect it. So it has to be caught before it's planted.

How do you catch it before it comes in? You watch what you let in. You have to watch who you talk to. You must watch what you listen to. Begin to regulate, and monitor these things. Whether you know it or not, subconsciously, you have no control over when and where that seed fully matures. The only thing that is certain is that it will mature and it will come out. Everything planted in soil, eventually comes back out. And when it is let out, it will be and do whatever it was planted to be and do.

Those seeds, can break up homes, hurt feelings, destroy relationships, crush spirits, and more damage. Some can lift spirits, encourage, guide and motivate later on. The truth is there's a 50/50 chance. And unless we learn to keep leashes on what's planted, we will never fully control what we cultivate, and we risk losing some of the very things, we've fought all this time to keep and protect.

This is why the bible tells us to avoid vain and profane babblings; This is why the word of God tells us to agree quickly with the adversary (when you agree with someone, more times than not, because that's what they wanted anyway, they just shut up); That's why we have to limit the conversation we have with the jealous folks; That's why we have to limit the conversations we have with the liars; That's why we limit the interaction with the thieves, the deceivers, the unbelievers, the HATERS, the doubters, the wolves and fowl...etc. These type of people plant seeds that grow to corrupt.

Friends and family, watch what you open yourself up to. Apply the scriptures. And if none comes to mind, here's one for you:

"And God will multiply the seed sown..."

Try to cultivate the seeds that He ministers to you. He multiplies ALL the seeds sown. BOTH good AND bad He's going to multiply them. And if you couldn't handle the seed planted, how do you think you gone handle the harvest that it yields?

Guard your heart saints and friends. It is not just defense from people and emotions. It's defense from spirits and demonical influences that seek to destroy us from the inside out. Mind the conversations you have. Mind the company you keep. If you don't, no one else will.

Peace be unto you... Peace be multiplied...

~Shalom~

Bible References:

Mt. 13: 3-9 Mt. 13: 24-40

Mt. 13: 18-23 Mt. 13: 38-44

Damaged But Not Destroyed

Last year Mikey got a new truck. Chromed out, tinted windows, sound system, tv's, and automatic everything. That truck was 'off da chain'! He pulled up and we all jumped in. We had no clue where we were going but we knew we wanted to ride in it. We ended up going to see his girl Wendy. He loved going to Wendys' place. She had red hair and the best quick meals he could ever ask for. Her dad name was David and he was a famous chef. Although we were all into that truck, to him it was "just a thing" as he would say. I admired Mikey's ability to wisely choose what to place value on and what not to, because that's something that I struggled with. But this truck was cool.

One day about four or five months after buying the truck, Mikey let his friend Bobby borrow it. Mikey was known for lending out his vehicles. Sometimes for months at a time, cause he always kept more than one. And he never thought twice about it. Bobby used the truck and wrecked it. Mikey thought for sure the truck was gone. After checking to see if Bobby was ok, Mikey went to look at the truck. He never once looked sad, or like he regretted letting Bobby use the truck. He had more of a relief look, seeing Bobby was ok. Mikey was just that type of guy. Mikey called his insurance company to have them take a look at it, to tell him what could be done.

A few days later, I could tell that Mikey was starting to miss that truck. Not that he valued it, but he had never lost anything before. I could only imagine how it would have made him feel knowing that the one time he did lose something, it was because he was trying to be nice and help out someone else. About two weeks later, the adjuster called and told him it was not a total loss. They said that the truck could in fact be repaired. Not only that, but it would be fully covered by the insurance. Relieved, Mikey exhaled and told the insurance company to do whatever they had to do to get it back up and running. And in about 30 days tops, Mikey was back in his truck and rolling again.

Nobody wants to see anything they've worked hard for just get taken away from them. Especially if it wasn't from some weird freak of nature like a hurricane, or flood, or something that big and out of their control. Mikey was happy not to have loss his truck. He washed and waxed that truck almost every day. Or at least it looked that way. He kept that thing shining. Everybody would complement him on how much he kept that truck's appearance up. So much that, soon after getting the truck back, Mikey opened up his own detailing spot. It quickly grew to be one of the biggest car detailing chains in the Triangle. If you ask Mikey today, had the truck never been in that wreck, he would have never gotten that business started. He would've been happy just washing his car every Saturday after he went and got his 5a.m haircut. But even in his misfortune, he made a fortune. It all worked out for his good in the end.

Quan's Corner

Jeremiah 31:31-34

" Behold, the days come, saith the Lord, that I will make a new covenant with the house of Israel, and with the house of Judah: Not according to the covenant that I made with their fathers in the day that I took them by the hand to bring them out of the land of Eygpt; which my covenant they brake, although I was an husband unto them, sayeth the Lord: But this shall be the covenant that I will make with the house of Israel; After those days, saith the Lord, I will put my law in their inward parts, and write it in their hearts; and will be their God, and they shall be my people. And they shall teach every man his neighbour, and every man his brother, saying, Know the Lord: For they shall all know me, from the least of them to the greatest of them: for I will forgive their iniquity, and I will remember their sin no more."

Ever felt like there was no way God would ever hear your prayer? Ever felt so far gone that you were afraid to approach God and ask him for forgiveness? Ever thought you've done so much wrong that there was no way in the world you could possibly do enough right to make up for it? Ever figured you've avoided God for so long that he probably aint even thinking about you anymore? I know I have. And I stand here today, a living witness, that God is still there, with his arms opened wide, waiting to hear from you.

Unlike some of the people we've come across in our lives, God don't write us off. God don’t look at where we are, and what we've done and consider us a loss cause. In spite of how we view ourselves sometimes, God always see us better than the way we see ourselves. He knew us before we knew ourselves, and yet he died for us anyway. He died for each and every one of us, just so he could have the right to tell us that, hey, "I saw you, and I still forgive you. I heard you and I still love you. I know you rejected me but I'm still here for you. "

You see the truth of the matter is that, things will never be the way they were when you used to talk to him on the regular. It can’t be. That truck will never look the way it did whenever Mikey first got it. Neither will it look like it did the night before he let Bobby use it. And that's ok. Because when the insurance company finally did get that truck back to Mikey, it was better than it was before it got wrecked. The spots; the scratches; The dent under the handle on the driver side; The back window on the passenger side that never rolled down; That stain on his seat from that he could never get out from that Pepsi he spilled; The pizza sauce that was smeared in the seat from the boys wrestling in the back seat after church that Friday night; the rubbing he heard when he went over bumps; the ticking he heard when he drove faster than 70mph ... all of that was gone. And although the truck was fresh even with all that, and even though Mikey was cool with those small glitches, the insurance company never knew about it. And when they restored it, they restored ALL of it.

God, being the great mechanic he is, with that all-seeing eye of his and that all-knowing mind of his, he too is ready to take you and make you better than you were before your crash. He wants to make you even stronger than that condition you were in, before you broke down and decided that you couldn't take any more. That little lying habit you had; that fornication demon you battled with; that lustful eye you had; that anger problem you had; that urge to fight you wrestled with; those insecurities you had when you were "trying to live right" the first time, are now gone and forgotten. If you think about it, you will see that the Lord has already started the work. He has already started making you feel uncomfortable in certain environments and situations you used to be cool in. He already made you feel funny around certain groups of people. And other groups have already started to act funny towards you. Things you used to do, and desires you used to have you no longer have and you can't figure out why... it's because Fully Restored Insurance Company has already started the repairs. He knows they haven't called you. He knows you haven't agreed to any terms. He knows you could really never repay him for anything he's done for you; but he started the work anyway. And he's not charging you a dime. All he asking from you, is that you talk to him. No, it's not like it was before, God promises to make it even better than it was before. You'll be better this time around. The relationship between you and him will be tighter this time around.

Brothers and sisters, God doesn't care what you've done. God doesn't see where you are. He doesn't care about how bad you feel. All he wants is for his child to come back home where you belong. God is asking for you to just speak to him again. It's been too long. It no longer matters what happened way back when. It makes no difference why you stopped talking to him. That's the past, and he wiped all of that away. Whether it was ten years ago, last year or last night... God forgot it all. And today he's sitting by heaven's phone awaiting your call. He's staring at the door to your heart, waiting for you to let him back in, so he can pick you up, dust you off, clean you up, and restore the relationship you've been longing to get back anyway.

Many of us have felt like damaged goods. Most of us are jacked up, nowhere near in good condition, but like Mikey's truck, we are not total losses. We are able to be and are currently being repaired. We are still usable. We are still precious in his sight.

I've come today, simply as a mail man to deliver this letter to you. With your scars, your faults, your short comings, your sins, your mistakes, your mess ups, slip ups, and screw ups, your wrongs, your dirt ... God still wants you. He can still turn this around. He's still knocking waiting for you to open that door, so he can come in. He forgives you. He misses you. And he still loves you, flaws and all. You may be damaged, but you are not destroyed.

God Bless you all

Making Budget

In the corporate world, most big businesses are run the same. They all have order of succession: management, supervisors, expenses, budgets, and profit margins. And all set up on pretty much the same system. Each year a dept is given a certain amount of money, let's say $350,000, for the budget this year. And if they spend the entire $350,000, they get a pat on the back and the budget for next year is bumped up to $500,000. The more they spend, the more they get the next year. The budget eventually gets so high, and they have taken so much money from the other departments, that the department that was being stripped, fails. And eventually, the failure in one part of the major company, affects the overall performance of the company. Soon, its expenses begin to tower its profits until they fall hard. Then they lay off the very people they once patted on the back for spending all the money. They are set free into the real world and they do what they know. They spend all the money they have, thinking that next year they will get more. But instead, they drive their families into a deeper state of poverty because of a spending habit that was instilled and encouraged by the life they lived outside of home. (And so we turn on the news and see the blue, white, and other collars all forms of suicide)

Now, another scenario with the same budget; The same $350,000 budget for the year. But this time the department only uses $280,000. The company pats them on the back but lowers the budget next year to $250,000. This department, this group of people, never maxes out the budget and every year the company pats them on the back. The budget in that department is now lowered and the money is spread around into other departments, as in scenario one, towards things like company vehicles, advertisements, employee raises, department bonuses, and etc. Here, eventually what happens is that the budget gets so low and the crew does such a good job with stretching and saving the money that the company realizes that it can function without the department as a whole. It requires little to no maintenance and monitoring that it will take care of itself. Then the employees of that department are let go (laid off) and released into the real world. Difference being, they made a living of saving money and making the best, and getting the most done with the least amount of resources. They do fine and bring their families out of poverty.

Quan's Corner:

After the recession the last couple of years, many of us have learned, if we didn't already know, how to stretch some resources. Be it money, food, ration out utilities, time, and/or energy, we all have learned to be more mindful of how we spend our resources. And it's a great lesson to learn, even under such unfortunate conditions.

The Bible tells us that God rewards those of us who are good stewards over what he gives us. He says things like, "to him that has, more shall be given him, and to he that have not, even that which he has shall be taken away." Or the parable of the men with the talents, the just steward, the woman with two mites, the woman with the empty vessels, the woman with the sick son… it's all over the Bible.

Just like in the corporate world, we too, are given a spiritual budget. And we have to stay within the allotted time and amount throughout the year. Every idle moment, every unproductive word, every vain conversation, every tenth of every increase, every seed ministered that was not sewn, every minute of prayer missed, every praise not given… it all has to be accounted for. And many of us tore that budget all to pieces. The difference here though, is that in God, there are no lay-offs. There is no poverty. There is no unemployment. The work accepted by every Christian is a permanent work. And thanks to grace and mercy that endure forever, we are able to remain part of His big company. And every day we wake up, we are granted another chance to get it right.

This year, you've received your spiritual budgets. You know what the Lord requires of you. Don't look at what you don't have yet; the test is to see if you are able to wisely utilize what you have, to see how much you really apply to the word already in you, before you seek new revelation. Surely, we all can find and name a place in our lives where we lacked, or a place where we can use a refilling or more of a certain thing. But true children of God, take what's given to them and learn to first maximize where they are. Not complaining about the problems we face, but rejoicing about the promise we live. No one is ever rewarded for crying, there are no trophies for complaining, there is no blessing for those who murmur. Someone once told me, "life's rewards go to those whose actions rise above their excuses."

As I bring this to a close, I'm reminded of a story in the bible. The story about a man named David and how his people, his family, and friends were terrorized by this giant. And about how the armies at the time would fall, trying to defeat Goliath. They had their fancy weapons, and shining armor. They mapped out their well planned strategies, and years of experience in war. Yet they didn't know how to use what they had. They were too busy complaining about what they didn't have. "If only we had more men..."... "We need a tank..." ... "If only we could..." ..." Only if there was a way..." ... And their excuses drowned their execution. And their problems were made bigger than their God. So they failed.

But David ... David didn't have much. He wasn't given weapons and armor. But on the way to check on his brothers like he was told to do, he found a couple of stones. And when he got to where God wanted him to be, with the heart and mind that, whatever God wanted him to do, he would make it happen. Long story short, David defeated this giant, by himself. With the budget he was given. He was given an order to go, a couple of stones and the strap of his shepherds' bag. David led himself and his family over a stumbling block that stood between them and their promise. And he did it, with his bag and a rock.

This year let's change the world. Let's bind the hands of the enemy in our lives. I don't know about you, but the enemy blinded me from blessings last year and I want them. Let's take back EVERYTHING that Joker stole from us last year plus interest! Let's do it without complaint. Let's do it without doubt, and without fear. Let's move without excuse and in excellence.

Let's Walk in Authority… Let's make this Budget!!....

God Bless

One Team, One Goal

"Lord if it be thy will, let this bitter cup pass me by..." As an act of recognition that in-spite of self will, the life of every son of man is written by the Lord, here we see even Jesus Christ himself yielding His life to God. Understanding His divine assignment, Jesus, who is God manifested in the flesh, that whatever He wanted Him to do, let it be so that He may reconcile the world back unto himself to get the glory out of His life. It's no secret that none of us "write our own ticket" with God, but instead we get in line for what He had already designed our lives to be.

Seeing this, we understand that as the head of the body of Christ, God in the position to have to lead the work with this fight against the devil. The head stores the brain, which is the control center of the entire body, as well as it is the most important position in the spirit of realm. Jesus, even as God, chooses not to go against order, realizing that by taking on a body (in that of Jesus) He also takes on another assignment. Not only as king of kings, but now as redeemer whose mission is to die for the sins of the world. So we see then, that it is God who gives instruction to the saints, for them to carry out their orders, so that collectively, the kingdom of God can dominate the kingdom of hell.

Quan's Corner:

If given the choice, which limb would you choose to amputate if it offended you? An arm? A leg? Perhaps a toe? When we think about losing a limb, one cannot decide which limb to get rid of. Reason being, that when it comes to us, placing value on things we deem priority or valuable, everything becomes equally important, as well as the obvious reason that each individual limb has its own duty. And it is because each limb has its own assignment for the human body to be able to function as a unit successfully.

Our body has a head that acts as the control center and a heart that pumps blood throughout the entire body, giving sufficient blood to each limb to function and function above normal level in extreme cases.

It is no different in the body of Christ. The church too, must follow the same principle. Often times, saints adopt the "that's not my job" attitude when it comes to laboring in ministry. Where in reality, the "job" of each saint is to see to it that the work gets done.

The pastor can't do it ALL. Neither can the deacon, nor the minister, nor the elders, nor the missionaries, nor the willing workers committee, or whoever else remains in ones church. Stop looking for titles do the work. And stop seeking titles for yourself if you aint working. People seeking seats are usually a good sign that they are underdeveloped. They are in fact babies or immature persons. They seek seats in high places, so give them a "high" chair (big baby). These people bring shame to the body of Christ.

Brothers and sister, just like any job: retail, merchandising, mechanic, technological engineering, fast food, and etc., teamwork is involved. And in most jobs, teamwork is often required for maximum production. Can you imagine if one person worked in a McDonald's? How long do you think they would stay in business? It takes ALL of the people of God to do the work of God. Each person maximizing their own place first in full force, is what brings about results that please God.

Notice that when one sense of the body malfunctions, the others get stronger. A person with poor eyesight can usually hear better than the average person. A deaf person will usually feel more vibrations than someone who can hear, and often times, can read lips better than your nosey aunts. And we have to be the same way. Getting to the point where we no longer compete with each other, but complement each other instead. When your shirt is nice, that's good, but when your kicks are fresh, it makes your shirt look even better. Let's help to maximize our collective goals even after we fulfill our individual goals.

Have you maximized where you are to properly advance the kingdom of God? Is God pleased with what He placed you over? Did you walk pass more people than you stopped to help? Let's maximize this thing out! Let's put a smile on the face of God!!

Peace be with you.

Swinging At Giants

In the art of war, armies are usually sent with the same mission. No commander and chief instructs an army to go into a place and kill all the woman. The dogs and cats aren't the focal point of those men. In fact, much like today with the US militaries in war were sent to dethrone the leader of that country. If foot soldiers were the expense, then so be it, but they were just that, expenses, not targets.

In all the old Kung Fu movies there were many good fighters. There was often a teacher that fought another teacher way back when, and now some student wants to avenge their master's death by fighting and killing that teacher. Usually, this student (now a teacher himself) sends students to infiltrate the gates of and kill the students of that teacher. The thing is that no matter how many students came against the teacher, he recognized they were too great to fight the students and they would only fight other masters. So instead of beating them up, the teacher would block and counter all their attacks until they realize it's useless and leave.

In the homes of most people today in this economy, there sits some type of opposition to financial freedom or hardships in the managing of finances. People are often found living paycheck to paycheck with just enough extra to put gas in the car. It'll be a stretch to say they'd even have enough left over to by lunch at work every day. But in all these cases the mentalities of the people are different; and even though some are "saved" and move in faith, and others are used to an "every man for themselves" type life style; even though some are old and some young, there is a common ground for them all. No matter how they money looking, one thing for sure is that if no other bill in the house get paid, that rent or mortgage gone get paid. Perhaps it's even the same way in your home. The phone may go out. The cable may get disconnected. They may have to eat peanut butter and jelly sandwiches or Ramen noodles for a couple weeks, but they gone keep a roof over their head.

Quan's Corner

Friends, all types of persons, in all kinds of situations, from all walks of life, go through things. Not everybody that goes through dies or gives up in the middle, but what gets most people is not just the fact that they go through something, but that they are often times feeling overwhelmed because it's normally more than one thing that attacks them at one time; or the enemy attacks them in more than one area at a time. I don't know about you, but I have my share of overwhelming experiences and they can be hard to manage sometimes. At least they used to be, before I remembered how to fight when I'm out numbered.

You see, growing up in "Dirty Jersey" *as we sometimes called it*, there were very few days that went by that we didn't have to fight. But I remember the first time I actually escaped and avoid getting jumped. My cousins told me what to do and I followed their instructions to a tee. They told me to spot the biggest or toughest one and hit them first. They told me to hit him and don't stop hitting him. It didn't matter how many hits I took from the others, I was told to make sure that I didn't allow that one, to walk away under his own power. I was told that when I met up with the rest of them the next day, they will be without that hard hitter and I would be able to run through the whole crew if necessary and it would be much easier. Believe it or not, I did just that.

Today I'm telling you guys, when the odds don't seem even; when the deck appears to be stacked against you; when you are attacked from five different areas at once; when it seems that there is no resting during this period; when you feel that your bell for this round just won't ring; when the pressure seems like it just aint letting up..... My advice to you is to focus on the big thing. As bad as you would want to keep all the thoughts and things from clouding your mind, you have to focus on the hard hitter. Identify it, and attack it. After you knock out the main thing, the confidence built from the victory of that battle, will generate the necessary momentum to defeat the rest.

Brothers and sisters you will get through. And not only will you get through, but you will come out a winner. You were built to last. You are destined to come out on top. And that which was destined from the beginning will come to pass. He said he watches his word and see to it, that it performs that which HE sent it to accomplish.

Bottom line is this... Keep the main thing the main thing. You don't have time to swat at flies when you're 'Swinging at Giants'!!

May the Lord God of Israel be your Strength

Is It In You?

I saw a man lying across the buffet aisle at golden corral. He had a terrible headache and he began to cry out in anger I asked him why he was crying? He said he was hungry and hadn't eaten anything all day. He said that's why he was lying across the bar. He said he laid on the chocolate fountain, he laid on the salad bar, and was now at the seafood bar but was still hungry.

I saw a football player sitting in a tub of Gatorade. He was breathing extremely heavy and his voice was close to gone .I asked him why he was so tired and seemed to be in a relaxed state or position. He said he had just gotten out of an intense practice and was thirsty. He said he had been soaking for about an hour, and if he didn't get something to drink soon, that he might faint.

I saw a sick woman crawling in a bed of pills. She was screaming that she was in extreme pain, and said she needed something to make the pain go away. I asked her why she was crawling around in the bed of pills. She said she spent the night in the bed of pills, but didn't feel any better at all. She said the pills were prescribed to her by her physician. She said he told her the pills would work within 8 hours but she has been crawling around in them for 36 hours now and don't feel any better at all.

I saw a young tourist at a gas station sitting in her car. She appeared to be stranded because her hazard lights were on. As I approached the car, the smell of gas entrenched me to the point where breathing became difficult. The smell was powerful and would make it hard for anyone to properly breathe there. Wanting to check on her, I continued forward. I noticed the car was drenched and still dripping but had rained in days. As I got up to the car the smell let me know it was gas. I knocked on the trunk so wouldn't startle her. As I approached she locked the doors and curled in her seat. I could tell that she was fearful. So I walked to the front of the car and talked to her through the windshield. I asked her why she was sitting there, and she explained she had no more money for gas and could not make it back home. She said she bought $80 worth and poured it all over the car but the tank is still on "E" and the car won't start.

Sound's foolish huh? Sound like a children's story written by Dr. Suese or someone. But the metaphors in these scenarios are very true. Journey with me into Quan's Corner.

Quan's Corner

The 1st scenario is likened to a person searching for the truth. They know the bible, can quote the quote the word verbatim, have listened to and memorized all the preacher's sermons line by line. Yet they continue to seek more. They look for more than God and His word. They seek more than revelation. The bible refers to the Word of God as the bread of life. It is the very the meat that feeds our spirits. Yet and still, with all that word around them, they have yet to get it in them. David said, "thy word have I memorized."??... NO!! "Thy word have I hid in my heart that I might not sin against thee." When the word is in you and not just on you (like your clothes are on you) then you treat one another right. You love your enemy. You pray for accusers. And your report is a much better one within and outside the walls of the church. These people are often found dabbling in other religions and are spiritually unstable.

The 2nd is likened unto a person that is eager to learn. They don't know the word and have not been able to catch on to the messages the preacher has been preaching. They still have a lot of questions about God, and the church and about Christians. The bible says that they desire the sincere mil of the gospel. It talks about the word of God being a well of water springing up into everlasting life. It talks about how rivers of living waters will flow out of our bellies. The thing is that even as bad as some of us want it, we refuse to get it in us. Instead we tend to sit, soak, and surround ourselves with it. Others of us surround ourselves with people that do have it in them to make us feel better, rather than drinking of that bitter cup ourselves.

The 3rd is likened unto a person who just refuses to operate in faith. These are those people who just won't accept the word of God as the full authority of Christ. They pick and choose what they believe out of it, but there is still some stuff they just can't get with. So God can't get with them. This type of person attempts to live a Christian life while only embracing a portion of what God requires, but we serve an ALL or NONE God. Either He is Lord *OF* all, or He will not be Lord *AT* all! So because they come to church but don't stop fornicating, they obtain mercy but not healing. They sing and dance but don't have a prayer life, so they have grace but no peace of mind. They dress up and be cordial but they talk about everybody in the church, so they make a lot of money but can never fully embrace love.

The last is likened unto a saint who feels like they are saved now. They been saved a long time and they "got it" now. They come to church every now and then. They may pay tithes when they have extra. They are strong in the Lord, all by themselves. They don't need friends. They refuse fellowship. They reject instruction. They watch the service on television or get the cd to listen to in their own time. They claim to read their bibles and pray in their home and feels that "it's just me and Jesus". They claim to have a "personal relationship with God". They and God just got a connection where He talks and deals with them directly. And they forget to assemble themselves daily in the house of God. They dismiss the coming together of the brethren with the breaking of bread. They miss out on the part where they are supposed to call upon the elders of the church to pray the prayer of faith. They totally do not understand corporate destiny. And they place their personal or individual desires and such, above that of the collective body of Christ. And much like that car they sitting in, they too are not filled. They don't get that boost, that refill, that push that us Christians sometimes need in order to keep going through our processes.

Saints and friends, it is not enough to have God on your mind. It is not enough to have praying people around you. It is not enough to attend a church service. It is not enough to be in the church. But you will only experience the complete benefit of this Christian walk when the church is in you or when the love of Christ is in you. It's not what you're in that makes you who you are. A bum in a suit is still a bum. A baby behind the wheel of a car is still a baby. An adulterer in a marriage is still an adulterer. A homosexual in a Bentley is still a fag! So again I say, it is not what you are in that makes you who/what you are, but it is what's in you that defines who or what you are.

This walk is an enjoyable walk to me, not because everything is great. It's not because nothing ever goes wrong in my life. It's not because everything goes as I plan for it to go all the time. We all go through. But those of us that endure and persevere not only go through, but we come out. I enjoy this walk because I am passionate about my purpose in the kingdom. I am fervent in the things of God. And it's easy to stay focused, to stay determined, and to keep fighting because it's in me!

Is It In You?

The Hype Man
(Move The Crowd)

Like most of you, I'm sure, there were many things that i enjoyed as a child. There were numerous things that caught my eye and held my attention. Over the years, my interests changed. Many of the things i used to care for, or that i found interesting, eventually just faded away. I couldn't even tell you what interested me about most of those things if you asked today. One of the interests that have not left me yet, is my love for music. That's my passion for the art of music.

I remember growing up watching videos and television shows that depicted concerts. I used to love seeing people perform on stage. Stage presence was one of the most difficult yet amazing qualities of any performer to me. The way they got all those people to give all their attention to them for extended periods of time was outright unheard of where I was from. The longest anyone I knew gave attention to anyone one person and actually listened attentively and behave, was the length of a court case. The only person we feared more than a judge was our parents growing up. And I say "our" parents, because back then we had parents over the neighborhood. They had permission to beat you in the stead of your own parent in the event of their absence from the scene of the offense. And even that was only until they returned, because they beat you again when they found out too. But the ability of a person to hold the complete and undivided attention of that many people for any extended period of time was a trait that could not be ignored.

As I got older my passion for music grew quite proliferate, and is still growing unto this day. I studied music and its positive and negative effects on people, society, communities, and culture as a whole. As I studied, and dug into the performance arena, I realized that it wasn't the performance that kept the attention of the crowd. It wasn't until after attending a concert myself that I realized that what kept the crowd involved was "the hype man". The hype man kept the crowd moving. The hype man got the crowd rowdy before the performer even got on stage to set the tone for the night. The hype man is what kept the crowd distracted enough to where they didn't get mad when someone bumped into them and kept dancing instead of fighting. They kept the crowd moving, even during the intermission. They gave the artist confidence and fueled the artists adrenaline to performer at a high and intense level. They kept the crowd interested in the performance. It was them that made the show run all the more smoother.

Quan's Corner:

The more I grow and mature, i realize that it's not only the singers, rappers, artists, magicians, comedians, or others that perform on stage, period, that have crowds. It is not only the basketball, football, baseball, hockey, tennis, players or athletes in general, that have fans and people watching them. It is not just the famous folk or celebrities that have large followings or people at them or even up to them in many cases. Most of us do as well.

Someone, somewhere, in some way or another, is looking to you as a role model, idol, mentor or just a "cool" person. Others look to you in envy and jealousy, despising your progression and counting on you to fall. Praying for your failure and preying on your joy. The bad thing about it is that you can't always identify them on your own right away. Sometimes the two are so even dressed, and so similarly appointed that they are almost identical to the natural eye, especially when we deal with people we love or have a tie to. The good news is, that's when serving an ALL-KNOWING God comes in handy.

In all fairness, we don't always feel that it's a good thing though. Sometimes we get mad at God. Sometimes we question ourselves and our own relationship with God. Ever feel alone? Ever feel like every time you turn around, someone you thought was cool with you, walk out on you or turn their back on you? Do you find that you feel alone more than you feel supported? Of course you do. Fact is, at some point or another, we all do. But it's not always a bad thing.

You see, what I've learned is that, today, you being the star you are, and having the influence you have in other people's lives, you too need a "hype man". You have a hype man. You have a very personal hype man strategically sent just for you. And that hype man not only acts as security, comforter, supporter, follower, guide...etc; but HE is also a way maker. Making the way and clearing the path for the betterment of your future. A true hype man is at his best when it comes to "moving the crowd".

THIS hype man moves everyone out of your way that is there to hinder you. HE moves everyone out of your camp that conspires with the enemy. He moves everyone back out of your inner circle that you moved in, in error because they were wolves in sheep's clothing. HE is fair enough to move those of whose potential you've hindered (in trying to help them of course) but in reality have only crippled them by not allowing them to walk on their own two feet. He moves..... And HE moves on your behalf.

There is no greater Hype Man than yours. Jesus is the Hype Man of choice; and by far, no one moves a crowd like He does.

So the next time you get into a position or situation to "step on stage", so to speak, don't you be discouraged by the size of the audience. When things look thin and the capacity is only half full, just know that your Hype Man has moved the crowd. Rest assured that the performance without that crowd, will be spectacular! Know that in due time, another crowd will be sent to observe, which it will produce more revenue, be more fun, and create a larger impact than you've ever dreamed.

Stay focused. Stop paying attention to the distractions,
And continue to perform like only you can.

May The Peace of God... Continue to rest, rule and abide over and in your life.... Always... Amen.

Swiper No Swiping

The Bible tells us that when a farmer sows, he sows then sleeps. And he waters the soil but he sleeps. Not waking in the middle of the night to see what he has grown this hour or the next, but he understands seed time and harvest. He believes that whatever he sowed/planted, will yield fruit, but in due season. And he busies himself until the harvest manifests itself. We all know that wheat doesn't get planted and harvested in the same season. We recognize that there is all the time that the seed is invisible under the soil. Then it breaks through and grows until it is finally mature enough to be useful. For one small seed is not nearly as useful as a bundle of wheat. That seed has the potential to be great. But not until it is nourished by the soil and water, then fed by the sunlight. But that doesn't mean that the farmer won't celebrate now.

You don't have to have fulfillment of the crop to announce the harvest. That farmer is going to make room, make prices, called the supermarkets and everything, even though those seeds are not yet manifested.

In the Bible an angel told Mary she would bring forth a son, and immediately she was filled with joy. She announced it and celebrated, even before she ever bore the child. Our mothers had to carry us for nine months, and she aint have to go check her "goods" every day to see if we had crowned, but she knew that in due time/season, she would conceive. Much like Mary and the farmer and our mothers, you too will bring forth if you nurture your potential. Whatever you do, don't give up!!

For us who aren't familiar with farming, a woman knows, most of the time, when she is pregnant before a medical examination ever confirms her pregnancy. Destiny is the same way. You "just know" that certain dreams in your life are going to become reality. And for those things, no one can convince you otherwise. You may not know when, why, or even how sometimes, but you "just know".

Now it may be months or years between the time you sensed it stirring within you and the time you see it happen in your life. Nevertheless, you realize that a waiting period is by no means strange, but part of the life cycle of every living thing. The only difference is, in farming the tomato season is known, and in birth the waiting period is in most cases known, but with dreams or destiny the time frame is known only by God. However, what is certain is that when God plants a seed within your heart, He prepares you for its full bloom.

And He ALWAYS makes it bloom at precisely the right time in your life. Not always when you want it, but always right on time. He waters you with the rain and storms of life. He strengthens you through trials and tribulations of life. He sends the root of your destiny deep, germinating the plans you thought you had for your life. And He stabilizes you well enough to stand on His promises alone, if need be, by removing the foundation of comfort you built for yourself with friends and family that aren't meant to be with you.

Quan's Corner:

In the process, you'll find that you don't always understand His ways and may become frustrated at times, with the wait. And this is, often times, why He waits so long. He gets you to the point that you exhaust all of your resources outside of Him, forcing you into a position to trust Him. This way He gets the full glory. Don't let your dream die though. You want a full grown dream come true to show the world. You don't want a pre-mature blessing. It will ultimately drain you more than it blesses you.

I want to ask you some more questions. Not so I can hear the answers, but for you to hear your answers as well. And after you've answered, hopefully it will make it a little easier to deal with the waiting period:

What did God promise you? What are you carrying? What is inside of you? Are you paying attention to the way it is growing and moving inside of you? Are you feeding it the positive energy it needs to grow properly or are those clouds of doubt and disbelief playing the spiritual umbilical cord to its being? What are you doing to prepare yourself for its fulfillment?

Maybe you are carrying a dream that you cannot birth right now. Maybe you are pregnant with unrealized potential. Maybe there is a gifting and purpose in you that must be properly nurtured before it can be enjoyed. Whether you are at the point where you should be buying a car seat, or painting the nursery, or preparing the baskets in the field for the gifts you cannot hold in your hand. Pay recompense to the unseen treasures that can only be marveled in the privacy of your soul. Dust off those dreams and begin to blow the dust off of prophesies you thought to throw away. Speak to the hope you tossed in the valley, and tell it to live again!!

So believe again my brother. Laugh again my sister. This is your season to birth, to give life to the miracle that dwells within you.

Be blessed my brothers and sisters. I look forward to rejoicing with you when your time comes.

Keep your dreams. Keep your focus. Keep your swag. Keep your faith.

May God give you Peace and Patience

The Rubber Band

I was in Ms. Steed's math class, at Henry E. Kentopp Elementary School. Even though her class seemed to last forever, no offense Ms. Steed, (probably only because I had her three times during the course of the day) school back then was fun. Almost all the teachers were cool. The principal was okay, and she knows who she is LOL. The office staff was great. Even the security guard Al and the janitors were mad cool. Back in elementary there were no cares. We saw the good in everybody. Somehow, I still managed to get myself in trouble.

I wasn't really a bad kid though. My grades were always honor roll. My character was always amicable. I had plenty of friends and countless family members. Even in all that I created an issue for myself, with trying to fit in. As well-known as I was, still every now and then I found myself still trying to "develop my own identity", and would do some of the stupidest things along the way.

I remember once getting in trouble for hitting this girl in the back of the head with a rubber band. She was a nice girl. She never bothered anybody. She actually ended up being one of my best friends in elementary school. Her name was Shaneefah M. She was cool peoples. But I, trying to be what I thought was cool at the time, decided to pop her with a rubber band. Of course I seen a side of her after that, that I never seen before. She got up and stabbed me in the hand with a pencil and broke off the lead in my finger in attempt to give me lead poisoning. I still got the lead in my hand to prove it actually, Lol. But I deserved it. We still friends twenty years later. But long story short, I got suspended.

I remember returning to school and having a rubber band ball in my cubby. The kids thought it was funny. I did too. The crazy part about it all was, I developed an interest in rubber bands. They became my favorite toy. I began to collect all different colors. I started making rubber band chains, rings, balls, and bracelets with them. I even remember sitting on the steps waiting for Mr. Stanley, (our mail man) to come just so I could get the rubber bands he kept on his wrist; *which at the time I used to think was just for when he came to our house.* It was pretty cool.

I used rubber bands for everything. I used them for papers, posters, my little brothers' hair, binding my cousins' legs together, as hand cuffs, made sling shots and other weapons, booby traps, decorations and even school projects. They became fascinating to me. It was a weird fascination for a child, I know, but I was no regular child. Ask my mom, I'm sure she'd love to share stories for days about my irregularities.

Quan's Corner

Today I don't hit people with them anymore, *not that often,* but I do still take interest in them. I collect them and use them most often as bracelets. They teach me now. Rubber bands serve as a reminder for me today. I'm older now, and my perception of life has changed. I no longer see rubber bands as weapons, but as testimonies. Rubber bands serve as a demonstration of my life as a child of God. They demonstrate the resilience of a true heir to the throne. They testify of the buoyancy of a real child of God. They depict how the patience of children of God everywhere is stretched, pulled and played with on a continuous basis.

They show how our tolerance is toyed with. Rubber bands display how elasticity is absolutely necessary to walk this Christian walk. They show how we are able to take the form of any obstacle that we find ourselves betwixt. They show how we are able to expand our thoughts around the word of God wide enough to grasp the most mind boggling events, and allow us to keep a grip on the toughest circumstances. They reminds us how, like rubber bands, we hold it together when things are wild and out of place.

But why? Why is it that we are allowed to be stretched so far? Why is it we are made to be bent out of shape and dis-fixed? Why would God allow any of His children to be pulled on and disfigured to the point where we become tight (tensed) and stiffened until it feels like we are about to pop? Then I watched. I begin to stop looking at what was going on in my life that bent me out of shape, and started paying attention to the fact that HE brought me out. I began to notice that I was better and stronger every time I went through something, every time I was put in a place where I was uncomfortable, every time I had to deal with someone or a group of people that pushed every button I had, I was wiser. I was now smart enough not to fall into the same positions again. I was now big enough to where the next time those obstacles came my way it didn't take as much for me to maneuver around them.

I began to take notice of my level and stature. I noticed that my disposition was no longer ill towards those things, simply because, like a rubber band, each time I was stretched HE let me go. He let me fend for myself so I could see the power HE had already placed within me. It gave me the opportunity to honestly measure my own growth. What I noticed, was that every time HE let me go in the midst of my stretch, it was not so that I would fall, but it was so, just like letting go of a rubber band in a sling shot mid-stretch, I would be catapulted to the next level I was destined to be on. I was not only stronger, better and wiser, but I was much further after my test, than I ever was before it.

Brothers and sisters know that, no passed test goes unrewarded. Understand that no progression or promotion goes untested. We serve a God that is omniscient. Just trust that no matter how things look right now, no matter how tight the situation, no matter how things feel right now, HE knows what's best for us. He doesn't only know how to get us where we are destined to be, but He knows the route to send us that will equip us the most for our destination.

Embrace the pulling. Welcome the stretch. Thank God for the tests. Rejoice during the uncomfortable stages, because it won't be long after, that we'll arrive to our next predestinated stop.

Keep ya head up....

The Quiet Storm

I remember being younger and living at home with my grandmother. Hard to think today about how long ago it was, yet I can still remember it like it was yesterday. Can you remember being a child? Do you ever recall losing a tooth? What were you told to do? You were probably told to gargle the salt water until the bleeding stopped. Rinse off the tooth that came out. Wrap it up and then place it under your pillow… probably something similar to this. At least that's what my grandmother told me to do. And as an effort to get me to fall asleep faster, she told me the tooth fairy would only come if I was sleeping. Anticipating the visit from "the tooth fairy", I'd fall straight to sleep. Never knowing what actually took place, never having actually seen the tooth fairy come, and never feeling a thing while I was asleep, I would wake in amazement seeing the tooth fairy had left me a whole dollar for one tooth!! That almost made me want to pull out all my teeth. LOL.. I said "want to"!

Remember believing in Santa as a child? Remember writing your Christmas list and mailing it off to "the north pole"? I do. I remember decorating the tree all nice, and leaving out cookies and milk for saint nick when he came. My grandmother would tell us to go upstairs and go to sleep. And I would rush off to bed knowing that, as long as I was awake, santa could not come. SO I never had a problem going to bed on Christmas Eve. I was anticipating waking up to a tree full of presents in the morning.

I remember taking long trips into the dark back country roads of North Carolina to see my grandmother. We call her Big Mommy. I remember having to ride in the car cramped up for hours until we got there. To pass time, we would try to distract ourselves by playing games and singing songs. I always liked to read the signs along the highway. But no matter what we tried to do to pass the time, that trip from New Jersey took forever. So we eventually fell asleep. And by the time we would wake up, we would be pulling up into Big Mommy's drive way. To me, I felt like I just dozed off for a couple of minutes. But it wasn't until I went to sleep, that the car seemed to get somewhere.

As humans, we have a natural tendency to have to put our hands to something. We need to feel like we took part in making something come to pass. And truth be told, we sometime slow, or even completely hinder the deliverance process or whatever we going through because we refuse to allow God to be God, and stay in our lane. At lease this is the case as long as we are awake.

Quan's Corner

I'm reminded of a story in the bible when Jesus and the twelve we on a ship. All the disciples were up on deck chillin, laughin and buggin out, chatting and crackin on each other. Jesus was in the bow of the boat sleeping. All of a sudden a storm arose out of nowhere. The boat was tossed with the waves. The waters were raging. And the lightning was flashing. The winds were boisterous and the disciples were frantic. They tried to steer the ship but couldn't. They tried to keep the water out but couldn't. They tried to hold on and not be tossed throughout the boat, but they kept losing their grip. So eventually, they went to wake Jesus to tell him what was going on.

Now Jesus immediately rebuked them. He fussed at them concerning their faith. He told them every attempt they made to get the ship back under control before they woke Him. Expressing to them his omniscience, he asked them why they had not learned anything from him yet after being with him as long as they had. Then he rebuked the winds and the storm ceased.

Now the funny thing about this story, is the reaction of Jesus after He got up. He appeared nonchalant. They even asked him, "master careth thou not that we perish?". They asked him did it even matter to him that they were stuck and sinking. But rather than answer them, he questioned their faith and asked them, why was it that they were doubting. He knew they weren't operating in faith. It was evident. Not by virtue of anything they did. They were skilled fisherman. They knew how to get the boat under control under normal circumstances. They did it all the time. It wasn't even because they had to wake him up. But it was evident because they were awake, instead of sleeping while he slept. What more comfortable sleep, than rest with God?

The Make Up Test

"OMG!! MY MOM IS GOING TO KILL ME!!!!" Lee said to himself after he received his chemistry test back from last week. He knew his mom asked him every day after work if he studied. He just kept telling her he did when he really didn't. Lee was used to the middle school classes and didn't realize that passing tests in high school without reading wasn't as easy as it was in middle school. He got a "D". And this exam happened to be worth 15% of his quarter grade.

Lee felt horrible. Not only was he going to have a tough time bringing this quarter grade up before progress reports, but his mother was going to give him the beating of a lifetime. Lee wasn't sure which one would hurt him the most.

Pleading with his teacher after class, Lee asked his teacher if there was anything he could do to get this grade dropped. "Unfortunately this exam was state mandated Lee, and the grades must be submitted for review by the board of education. I'm sorry but the results from this test are not mine to tamper with. I have to turn them in." Lee dropped his head as a lump grew in his chest. This was a hard one to swallow for him. Even though his mom didn't know anything yet and would probably not find out for about another month or two, he was still afraid. "Thanks anyway Mr. Cogate." Lee said as he turned around to leave the class with his chin almost dragging the floor. "These scores have to be submitted on Monday. If you are interested, I'm giving a make-up test on

Saturday at 9a.m. It turns out that a few of you did very poorly on this test and I felt it only right to retest you guys. So if you want…" Lee interjected "I"LL BE HERE AT 8a.m.!! THANK YOU SO MUCH!! I'm going home to study right now!!!" Running out the door, Lee lifted his head and went to his next class thanking God for making a way of escape for him.

Saturday came and Lee stayed after for about 45 minutes while Mr. Cogate graded his paper. "B+" said Mr. Cogate. Lee leaped for joy. He thanked his teacher again and ran home just in time for lunch. Mom was making Jamaican beef patties. Which happened to be Lee's favorite. A good beef patty with some cocoa bread and cheese was enough to make him go crazy!!

Quan's Corner:

I remember the days we had make-up tests. I was probably just as excited about it as Lee was. I too, much like many of you all were too I'm sure, was the type that didn't study like I should. I relied on prior knowledge to get me through all current tests. I will admit that most of the time, I was fine doing so. I aced most of my tests. I rarely failed. But there were times I did fail. And the make-up saved my G.P.A. and my backside.

Today, although I'm finished with school, I still find myself tested on a regular basis. Most people find themselves tested as well. God tests us and Satan temps us. I know there are times I want to slap some people. Times I thought to steal and times I did steal. Times I sinned against God and my brothers and sisters. Be it lying, hanging with the wrong crowd, stealing, cheating on my diet, fighting, cussing, trusting the same people that did me wrong over and over, drinking, smoking, fornicating... or whatever else I was tested with, the tests came often. And truth be told, unlike school, in life I probably failed more tests than I passed. And I should have surely flunked this class called life.

When I think back on how things went in my life, I find myself scratching my head. I honestly don't know how I got through many of the seasons I went through. But the more I study and the more I look back to reminisce, the more I understand. I see now that God is indeed the instructor if this school of life. And seeing the mess I got myself into so many times, he saw fit to throw me a make-up test every now and then. And I'm eternally grateful for them.

Ever wonder why you find yourself going through the same things over and over and over again? Ever find yourself in the familiar predicaments? See situations on repeat in your life? Find yourself dealing with the same kind of man or attracting the same kind of man every time you think of entering a relationship? Have you been fired from more than one job for the same thing? Do you find yourself making the same excuse more often than you meant to? Feel like you've messed up your life so bad that there is no way to fully recover from all the mistakes you've made?

Brothers and sisters I come to you with good news. It wasn't that your life was just meant to go a certain way. It's not that you were not meant to be happy or be with the person of your dreams. It's not that you are under some sort of generational curse. All this time you were worried about how to get out. All this time you were wondering why you keep starting over in life. All this time you thought you were going to go crazy if you seen or did whatever... just one more time. It was Mr. God, giving you a make-up test. He could've taken your life. He could've blew out your life candle in heaven. He would have been justified in letting you get killed out there in them streets. But HE saw enough in you to give you a make-up test.

Study your material. Learn from your mistakes in this life. Try not to make the same mistake over and over. Take time to talk to your instructor. Get on your knees or go to your secret prayer closet and let the word of God tutor you. If you haven't already done so while reading this, take this time to lift your hands and give thanks to your instructor for not failing you. Thank HIM for not kicking you out. Give HIM thanks for allowing you, even against the rules, to take The Make-Up Test.

Keep the Dirt Out of Your Eyes

Ever been lied on? Ever been talked about? Ever been miss represented? How about misunderstood? Have you been saved long enough to have been in a position where you were innocent and couldn't prove it? Of course you have. In fact we all have. All of us have had, at one point or another in our lives had someone who had some "dirt" on us. We've all had someone to take that dirt and try to bury us in it. They even succeeded sometimes. It was to the point where anytime anyone walked by us, all they seen was the dirt. People wouldn't even attempt to get to know us because the stain of what they heard about us was too bad. They didn't even care about finding out the truth. They just went by what they heard and left us under the dirt to suffocate. Others added to the dirt to make sure we would never come out.

The problem was, none of them realized that under the dirt life still exists. Most rivers and/or streams at some point run underground. Some electrical wiring is done underground. Water lines and pipes are driven underground and we walk over them every day. There are many railroads that are run underground. There are highways and tunnels that have to go underground to circumvent bodies of water. Not to mention the plant and insect life beneath the surface. Even the bible tells us that Christ is unto us a well of water, springing up into everlasting life. Well, the only way to spring up is to come from below. The bible also says, that out of your belly shall flow rivers of living water. You get the point. Things under that dirt weren't all bad after all.

Now let's talk about seeds. In order for a seed to grow it requires a number of things. We being seeds require also the same types of things to grow. Pressure, heat, water, and "dirt" also referred to as "soil".

We have all been under some type of pressure before at least once in our lives. Whether it was at school for a final, at work with a deadline, at home with last minute shopping or bill paying; at some point we all have. Truth be told, whatever we were pressured with at that moment felt like the heaviest burden in the world.

We have all been in heat. Whether it's been fire put under us by someone attempting to help us get to the next level. Heat put on us by someone trying to kill our reputations, or just being in the heat of battle as Christians. At one point or another we have all felt the heat.

We have all been in water. For some of us it was deep waters we were treading in. Others of us were dancing on the water beneath the thin ice we were skating on. Many of us were just in situations that got in too deep. It may have even been us trying to hold on to our salvation when hell and high waters came. Whatever the case, we've all been in our fair share of water.

We have all had some dirt thrown on us before. Be it out there by someone else to kill us. Maybe we put it there to bury the old man in us. Even if we were in the process of giving a strong hold the benediction, we've all experienced it.

Quan's Corner:

The next time you come across someone who tried to suffocate you with dirt, thank them. Let them see the finished or older (cause some of us aint finished yet) product of the seed that they tried to destroy.

Recognize that they did give you a proper burial and when you used the word "dirt" you got angry. When you heard the word dirt you were bothered. When you heard the word dirt, you wanted to retaliate. However, as we matured into our Christendom, we recognized that dirt was only "fertilizer" and it was only for our benefit. Fertilizer was required for us to grow. It helped us take route (root). It helped us grow strong. It kept the temperature right for maturation. It only pushed us further into our destiny. It only made us better. The fertilizer that they thought they were using to harm us, only made us stronger... you get the point.

In life we are going to get fertilized. We are all seeds until we die; even after we germinate, we still have to be in good ground to continue to grow properly.

Our only task is to keep the dirt out of our eyes. Don't become blinded by the attacks of the enemy. Don't become side tracked by the situations and circumstances that arise. Stay focused. Keep your eyes on the prize. Through it all, learn how to continue to press towards the mark of the prize of the high calling in Jesus Christ.

God Bless you all. Let’s brush the dirt off. Thank God for the fertilizer. Lets live for God without excuse and in excellence!

Keep Your Helmet On

Coming up my cousins and I would not be in the house much. Unlike children today, we knew life outside. We weren't stuck in the house on a wii, xbox, or ps3. We were out building club houses, tree houses, playing freeze tag, man hunt, hide-n-seek, even hop scotch and jumping rope with the girls on the block. By the time we came in the house we were tired. We ate and talked about all the fun we had that day. Those were little things that kept us close.

Although we didn't watch much television, part of the reason was because we didn't have cable, but from the channels we did have, we would all gather every Saturday morning and watch this one cartoon. We never missed an episode of x-men. We, like most children, fathomed what it would be like to have super powers. We each had a favorite character. They each had one of the heroes as their favorite. Wolverine because he could heal fast and could not die. Storm because she was able to manipulate the weather. Night crawler because he had the ability to teleport anywhere he could envision. Morph cause he was a shape shifter and could turn into any of the characters he wanted to be. But me, I chose a villain. My favorite character was the arch enemy of the heroes.

My favorite mutant was a man by the name of Magneto. They thought I was lame for that. After all, he was just a human magnet. Truth is, I didn't even know why I liked him. Something about him was just "cool" to me.

Often times we would see the leader of the heroes, his name was Professor X. He had the power to read minds and manipulate thoughts. He was pretty much "the man" cause he could make you think whatever he wanted you to think, or relive any moment in your life that he wanted you to. Everybody was afraid of him. Everybody that is, except Magneto. You see Magneto wore a helmet. And the helmet kept the professor from penetrating his thoughts. So the professor couldn't control him. And that was good for me. Although Magneto never won, he never lost either. They would just part ways until the next time. He had a great counter, and was the only mutant able to avoid being controlled by Professor X.

Quan's Corner

Today the world is full of people like Professor X. Everyone, including the devil and his army, seek to manipulate your thoughts and control your mind. Everyone, for one reason or the other, wants to get into your head. They seek to play mind games. And whether it's a shrink, a lawyer, a friend, a family member, or just someone going around talking about people in an attempt to sway the opinions of and turn people against each other, they all seem to succeed in some way.

Even I fall victim to it from time to time. I fell for the "he say/she say..." I formulated opinions about people, whether they did or didn't do anything to me, based on hearsay. I've let folks in my head thinking I was venting, only to find out later that I was pouring out my inner most thoughts to a friend of mine enemy. And in some cases, even my enemy themselves.

One of the most powerful attacks the enemy has, is the attack on our mental. If he can cause you to lose focus, If he can make a noise in one room of your home (mind) and distract you for even one second, if he can get you to doubt just a little bit of the prayer that you just prayed... If only he can find some way to cause you to lose momentum in one area/aspect of your life, then he can enter through the windows of your mind to destroy you. Death, sickness, poverty, relationships, marriage, friendships, kids cutting up, family isn't there, boss getting on your nerves, people acting a fool... are all distractions. Don't fall for them.

Saints and friends, learn from Magneto. His defense against the enemy was not his ability to counter attack with a great and mighty blow. It wasn't a giant fireball he could throw at them. It wasn't that he could manipulate winds and elements, or move lightning fast. He didn't have to sneak up from behind, or even plan a perfect strategy. He didn't have to turn invisible or set a trap; all he had to do, was get into uniform, Although he wasn't as blessed, equip, and prepared as you are, seeing how you have the full armor of God, he did have a helmet. It turns out that helmet was the key to his greatest defense. His greatest defense was his ability to remain focused and keep people, situations, enemies, circumstances, feelings, emotions, and distractions all out of his head. Truly a focused saint is the devil's worst nightmare.

Are You Focused?

Put down those weapons of carnality. Stop thinking of ways to go around your enemy's camp. All he has is the power of suggestion (through temptation and manipulation). Put on your uniform and walk right through it. Keep your eyes on the prize. Keep ya guard up. Keep the faith. Keep fighting, And most of all..... Keep your helmet on!!

God Bless

The Liquid Prayer

One of the most powerful weapons of warfare granted a Christian is prayer. More so than any portion of the full armor of God, prayer is the "one hitta quita " of the spirit realm. And it is by far the enemy's worst nightmare.

It is the very bridge that connects the kingdom of God and the soul of the sinner. (They that call upon the name of the Lord shall be saved.) It is the condition to our eternal communication. (IF my people would humble themselves and pray, and turn away from their wicked ways, THEN will I....) It is the hour where we are closet to our Heavenly Father. Even Jesus recognizes this. (And He sits on the right hand of the Father, praying in intercession...) It is our "magic wand", our scepter, our telephone operator to God.

I was taught that there were four types of prayer; the prayer of supplication, thanksgiving, intercession, and the prayer of faith. All of which leave very lasting impressions on the head of the enemy. The blows of each, severely damage the kingdom of hell. But none of which, I believe, delivers a blow like the one that was left out which is the fifth type of prayer.

The only thing about prayer that the enemy can use as an opening is the fact that he too can hear it. It is the fact that whatever he hears during that prayer provides him with the fuel and focal point of his next attack. He hears where you need help.

He hears where your weak area is. And he sends legions of demons, imps and devils to attack that area. That's why sometimes, it seems like as soon as you pray about something and you get up feeling light, like a burden has been lifted, here comes the devil (we call it the test)..

But the 6th and final type of prayer eliminates that handicap. It eliminates the excuses the apostles had, that they knew not how to pray as they ought. It shuts the theologians up with their fancy linguistics and theological terms that make us common folk ashamed to pray behind them, out loud at least. And it's because this prayer uses no words. It involves no scripture quoting or memorization. It is not a bunch of rebukes. There is nothing supernatural so you don't need the Holy Ghost to pray this prayer. The prayer consists of only a simple action. One that comes natural when we go through beyond what we feel is our limit anyway. It is what I refer to as the liquid prayer.

Quan's Corner :

Anyone who is anybody in Christendom, and have been in this a while can witness that there are times that we just don't feel like praying!.. We just tired of sending up countless prayers all the time over and over. (especially when it seems that they aren't getting answered).. If you don't know what I'm talking about you haven't been saved long enough yet. And anyone who has lived life for a little bit now can attest to the fact that life sometimes deals us some messed up hands. There are times where we don't even know if God will hear us if we pray. There are times when things seem to come from everywhere too fast all at once. So fast that we cannot catch our breath, where we cannot even talk about what's going on. Not even with God.

In both cases, Christian or not; saved or unsaved; the common ground there is the hard time we both have verbally expressing how we feel at the time. Whether it's because we can't fully describe what's going on or we just, honestly, don't know what the heck going on. The meeting place or crossroads, if you will, is this very personal type of prayer. A prayer I call, "The liquid prayer".

Confused, not knowing if it's too late, not knowing if God is still there, not knowing what to do next, feeling that the load has become too heavy to carry on our own... we all cry. When the words we seek just don't seem to come to mind, we cry. When fussing, arguing, fighting, and cussing (saved and unsaved!!) just aint enough we cry. When the load is unbearable we cry. When the smoke gets so thick that we can't see our own way out, we cry.

We cry, and the enemy is confused. He hears no words. He has no clue where to attack next. And God, knowing the very source of every tear, hears the words that every tear conceals. Then He grants the request to lighten the load. And thus fulfilling the scripture that, "they that sow in tears...." . I'm glad I serve an all knowing God!!!

Stay encouraged. Know that God hears both the spoken and non spoken prayer requests. And as long as we are alive, the one prayer that demands the immediate attention of God, is the liquid prayer. He can't ignore it, because that moment is too intimate to HIM to pass up.

Know that God hears you. And when your request is made known unto God, He WILL deliver.
Pray on Prayer...

Peace be unto you...

It Starts At Home

The bible teaches that Jesus was born of a virgin. The virgin's name was Mary. Mary was engaged to a man named Joseph. It tells us that, although Joseph is the accredited father of Jesus, that Jesus was in fact the Son of God. (No Maury DNA results needed there!!) The book of Matthew 13:54-58, tells us that after returning from a city, Jesus went back "home". There, He taught a couple of lessons at the synagogues, and baffles the minds of some of the wisest people in that town. But then, ironically enough, because Jesus was able to astonish those who called themselves wise, they began to persecute Him.

They began to put away wisdom, and deal with him as common. The scriptures talk about how they "claimed to know His mother", and Mary's husband, at the time, Joseph (Jesus' dad) and they began to treat Him as they were accustomed. They not only spoke to Him directly, but begin to speak to the locals concerning him, casting doubt in the minds and the hearts of the people. Speaking of how there were those who grew up in Jesus' neighborhood. They began to call out those who played with James, Joses, Simon, and Judas, who were the brothers of Jesus. Likewise, they called out the women who played with His sisters. Some of which had parents who probably looked down on His parents because they were at a higher social status than Joseph and Mary.

They kept spreading these thought and ramblings until, like most words and thoughts, their words formed thoughts in the minds of the entire town. And so the bible goes on to tell us that Jesus did not many miracles there because the people there no longer believed in Him as the Son of God. So He laid His hands on a couple of sick people and healed them, then He bounced.

After he left, He called the twelve and began to send them out. Showing them they possessed the very same power He did because of their willingness to follow and obey. He began to teach them how to walk in authority as children of God, even as He was.

Quan's Corner:

This is a very popular or well-known story in the bible, and has become very prevalent even in our homes today. And I'll tell you how in just a moment...

What I want you to get from this though, is not the fact that He wasn't received. Not the fact that his friends, and even some family members didn't believe. Nor could they grasp the concept long enough to understand who He was, even though the rest of the world did. But what I want you to see, is that it didn't stop Him. Out of comfort, or to the deny the hurt of rejection, He could have easily blocked them out and said, "forget them", and move on to the next city. But realizing He had a work to do there, in that city, He found another way to reach them. (LISTEN TO ME LEADERS)

The book of Mark, the sixth chapter, holds the same account of the rejection of Christ in His hometown. But what Mark goes on to say that Matthew omits, is that He began to empower others to do it for Him. You see, the disciples (at this time they were not yet recognized as apostles) weren't from around there, so the persecutors had nothing on them. It was easier from them to receive from men who, they had no prior history of. (This is probably why new pastors can come set up a church in your city and begin to proselyte your members. They are too familiar to your voice that they no longer hear the voice of God. And instead of raising up a church to speak the same word with another voice, you forget the mission and think about the money or prestige.) But He sent them to His hometown first, knowing that if those around Him or those that were closest to Him (earthly) didn't get it, or were unable to benefit from who He was, that His work would have been for naught.

Friends, if nobody else is blessed by the changes you make... If nobody else understands exactly what it is God is doing in your life... If no one else receives what god has placed in you to bless them with, "HOME" has to. And because Jesus realized that, He was unselfish enough, and Master enough to remove himself and break himself, putting a little of himself into each one of the twelve, giving them the power He had, which was nothing more than the knowledge that demons and devils were subject to all of the children of God. And that they too were gods. And he sent them on their way.

We can never get too enmeshed with the idea that not everyone will understand. Neither can we be entangled by the ideology that this is not a popular walk, that we overrule the message with the messenger. No leader, ANYWHERE, no matter how well he can present an argument, has the ability to obtain heaven's backing teaching anything contrary to what the bible teaches. Not focusing on one scripture and presenting your personal opinion as the word of God.

The thing that makes a pastor a great man of God is not his ability to deliver a message with tuning, using theological terms, or having 7 degrees on the wall in the office. It is in fact his ability to lead a flock of sheep long enough for them to grow and find pasture even when he isn't there. The ability he has to train his congregants to read the word of God for themselves, not to disprove what he teaches, that would be foolish, but to confirm the message delivered across the pulpit with the inerrant word of god which is the more sure word of prophecy. The bible backs up itself all day long. It doesn't need an attorney to prove its case. It doesn't need a translator to say what it meant. It means exactly what it says. And it backs itself.

Likewise, what makes a teacher a good teacher, or what makes a trainer a master, is not how many of his students he can beat up... or how many more words he can spell than the students... but the ability to teach and/or train long and effectively enough for them to become teachers and trainers. I believe that any teacher that has not trained a student who has surpassed them, is not yet qualified to be a master teacher.

Don't be selfish with your mission. You want to get your family saved? You want to reach your old buddies from around the corner, or down the street? You want to know how to effectively give back to your community? Take the knowledge you have now, and instill it in someone else. And teach them to do likewise.

How many time have you said, "If only I knew then what I know now"? How much better off would your neighborhood had been had you had that knowledge? How much better would things have gone in your house? How much further would your generation be...?

Don't let another generation come up without the knowledge that you didn't have at that age. Find somebody to mentor. Find a heart that's good ground, and plant a seed of belief. Half of the generation beneath us doesn't even know what it is they want to be when they grow up. Let alone, have any hope for a positive future. Give it to them. And teach them to give it to those around them.

It starts at home....

May the favor of God be with you as you reach back for the lives of those you left.

"And the Lord said, Simon Simon, behold Satan hath desired to sift you as wheat: But I prayed for thee, that thy faith fail not: and when thou art converted, strengthen thy brethren."

~ Luke 22.31-32 ~

Wet Walls

Just the other day someone called me. They called themselves congratulating or encouraging me. They started saying things like "congrats on the new business taking of." "That's a nice truck you got." "You and the lady look like y'all doing well." "I saw you in the $100 offering line, so God must be pouring it out "That suit you had on Sunday was nice, must've cost you a grip." "Heard you are in the process of building your own home from the ground up, sure wish I had it like that." And they just went on and on about all the blessings they seen in my life (or at least what they thought they saw), but the more they talked the more I began to hang my head. I began feeling bad. I looked up towards heaven and began to pray. "Lord I wish I felt like they think I feel…". The truth of the matter was that I wasn't excited at all about what was going on in my life. In fact, I was to the point where I was questioning whether or not Got was still there. Isn't it crazy how the perception that others have of you can be so far from the perception you have concerning yourself?! To make matters worse, that's not even the craziest part of it. What will absolutely blow your mind is the fact that they'll become jealous, just like the person on the phone was. They envy a person who actually feels like they are on the verge of throwing in the towel and backsliding.

Speaking of backsliding, in writing this piece, I'm reminded of a story in the bible very similar to how I was feeling. One that's probably familiar to everyone reading this, which will save a lot of time because I don't have to retell it. And that's the story of the escape from Egypt across the Red Sea, and the miracle of God parting the waters.

You see, when we read this story today, we rejoice. We say things like. "Man, if I would have saw something like that I would have NEVER doubted God again!" or "God was really with them, how could they possibly complain!?" or "How they gone say they thirsty and murmur about that when they just walked across a sea!?" or "They on dry ground, in the MIDDLE of a sea and still doubting God!!?? " People who retell this story often point out all the great things about the miracle, and all the hearers rejoice! The people that were there, however, weren't rejoicing at all.

Can you imagine walking in a crowd of about million people, trying to escape from Pharaoh and his army? Now this isn't anything organized, like a million man march or something. They aint even know where they were going. Now, you can't run because you will trample over each other. Some of the people there were tired. There are sleepy children and restless babies amongst them. You have to carry and push folk along the way. Aint no running at all because it's too crowded, so you're walking; and the enemy is gaining up on you. Now remember the bible tells us that, Pharaoh and his men were on their best chariots ("*chosen chariots*" Exodus 14:7) knowing that when they catch you, they are going to kill you and your family. Can you imagine that? If you not in a state of shock yet, wondering how in the world we are leaving these chariots on foot!!?? Then let's imagine a little further ...

Imagine now, walking at the bottom of the sea floor, and all you see on either side of you is 300 feet of wet wall (WATER!) that is somehow held back. In the back of your mind you know that at any given moment, these walls can collapse and you along with a million or so comrades of yours will be swallowed whole never to be seen again. You got sharks, and piranhas, barracudas and other great fish swimming at you full speed, and are halted only after smashing into this invisible force field. You cannot sit here and tell me that your thoughts are "God made a way of escape. "! No! Instead you are tip toeing like, "I know dog on well he don't think I'm going to walk in between those walls!!" You have got to be plum crazy! But the enemy is gaining on you, so you can't stop. You closing your eyes and praying all the while looking at Moses like, "Nigga you sure God said go this way!!??" You get my point.

Quan's Corner

I don't think there can be a more frightening method of rescue than this. Being delivered will not always feel like deliverance. From the outside, when people see you they just see progression. At the same time, you see the wet walls surrounding the escape route that you know, God has provided for you. There is nothing comfortable, nor familiar about this deliverance process. You can't see God through these high waters. You can't see how far you got until you get to the other side of this sea, because your eyes are shut so tight because you trying not to panic out of fear looking at this path. You can't hear HIS voice over the sound of the enemy's chariots getting closer and closer to you. All the while in your mind you're shouting "LORD WHAT"S GOING ON!!??

Saints and friends, there is nothing fun about new ground and deliverance. It's not always an easy and comfortable process, but you have got to know that God is still there. Even in the midst of everything that is going on, you are not alone walking through what looks like your impossible situation, God is still there! I know it doesn't always look like it. I know you can't always see Him but He's right there. He paved the way at the beginning of the process. He is protecting you in the middle of it. Trust and believe that He's awaiting your arrival at the end. He is omnipresent. Before He allows the enemy to catch up with you, both heaven and earth will pass away.

Sure we're not chased by Pharaoh today, but even in our cases the enemy moves faster than us. Who are these enemies? The liars, the thieves, the back biters, bills, gossipers, layoffs, taxes and fees, rising interest rates, temptations, the streets, beautiful women (for the men), (and for the women) handsome men, a failing economic system, false prophets, deceitful politicians, sometimes even friends and family members, etc... And they move fast. It seems like you just crawling and they are gaining on you, but they haven't caught you yet. They've sought to destroy you and tare you down, and get you to throw in the towel all these years, and you're still standing!! That has to be GOD!! The reason we know it's God, is because you know just like I know (and I don't know your situation) that nothing you do can get you out on your own. It takes God to get us out of the mess that, some of us, have made with our lives.

Since you can't see beyond those wet walls, let me tell you what the aerial view shows. God is manipulating everything around you. He is moving people who don't need to be in your life, out of your life. He is closing doors that lead to the enemy's camp that you planned to walk through unknowingly. He is opening doors for you that you would have never dared to even approach, let alone open yourself. He is removing the road blocks from in front of you and building bridges over every cliff before you and closing the walls on the enemies behind you. He is breaking the wheels of the chariots that seek to destroy you. He is forcing the hands of the enemies that seek to hurt you, open up and bless you. Although you can't see it, as long as you keep walking forward, *by faith now, because walking by sight at this point will kill you,* you will reach the promise that God has placed ahead of you.

Stay encouraged my brothers and sisters. I know whatever you're going through right now doesn't feel like a rescue mission, but those wet walls aren't there to hurt you. They are there to help you, by luring the enemy into your path of escape. Keep walking. Walk by faith. What you see if you walk by sight will discourage you. Walk by faith!! God is right there with you. He hasn't brought you this far just to leave you. Let the outsiders continue to be jealous. They don't know what it looks like on the inside. But the words they are speaking into your life by accident, "you're on dry ground", "heard you got a raise", "you must be happy" ...etc... will only speed up your deliverance process.

Peace be unto you all. Peace be multiplied.

Victory

Private Braveheart is a US marine. He has been faithfully serving on the force for a little over eight years now. Yesterday he got a call from his staff sergeant. He told him that they would be going to war today. In all of his years of serving, Braveheart has never actually had to go to real combat. All of the action he had was from drills and practice stimulations, so he was afraid. Seeing him afraid made the members of his platoon afraid as well. You see, Braveheart was the toughest man on base. He had been known for hospitalizing men in the MBA (Military Boxing Association). He was an undefeated force to be reckoned with. Naturally, when the soldiers saw the fear in the eyes of their hero, they all feared for their lives.

Today they went to battle. Seventeen hundred armed men went out to face an army of about twenty-three hundred. Braveheart fought his butt off trying to stay alive. The men were taking a beating. Of the 1700 men that went out, only 300 of them were alive to fight. The enemy had just over 800 men left. It didn't look good for team USA and they knew it. The men all had tears in their eyes as they rounded up their last bit of ammunition. Some of the men started to pray. Many of the men sought to find cover so they could write letters to their loved ones back home. Some of the men went into hiding while others of them simply played dead. Braveheart knew they couldn't possibly last much longer, so he too took cover.

Braveheart took out the radio and began to call for backup. No one responded. The army was in Iraq and Iran, the Navy was in Kuwait and Russia, the air force was over in Jerusalem protecting Israel, the Holy City. After 48 minutes of trying to reach US backup Braveheart began to give up.

Loading his rifle for what he prepared to be his last time, Braveheart dialed for help one more time. To his surprise, this time, there was a voice on the other end. It was the Korean air force. Braveheart quickly identified himself as ally, explained the situation and gave up his coordinates. The Korean forces took flight immediately, saying their ETA was 27 minutes. Braveheart's face lit up as he exhaled in relief. Korea was 1,900 soldiers deep. This was the air force alone. Braveheart just knew that there was no way they could lose now.

Joining his fellow marines in battle, Braveheart sprinted from his hole. Laughing and joking as if he was on some sort of video game, Braveheart fought with a smile on his face. Seeming to have found this new strength and zeal, he fought like he had been out there a thousand times before. His crew looked at him scratching their heads, wondering how he could be so happy at a time like this. They thought to themselves, *how could he smile when the battle didn't seem to be in you favor at all*? Many of them got mad with him, believing he thought he was in some sort of training simulation or video game. They thought it to e a way to carelessly give up the location of the others. What they didn't know, was that, although they had not arrived yet, was that he was confident now, because he knew that help was on the way…

Quan's Corner

The word "victory" in and of itself indicates that there had to first be some sort of battle or struggle. It makes no sense to need to gain victory over a situation or adversary if indeed they posed no threat or opposition.

We need victory on this here battlefield. Right here where we are fighting for the Lord each and every day is where we need victory most. We, much like Braveheart and his men, feel out-numbered by the demons that come against us. We see our fellow laborers in the gospel fall left and right, day in and day out. Some fell to fornication while other fell to adultery. Some fell to drugs while other were possessed and driven by greed. Some fell to homosexuality and others just to the way of Cain or the ways of this world. The more of our brothers and sisters fell, the weaker our strength in numbers looked. It doesn't help that we can't physically count how many demons fall during this battle so they always appear greater in number.

Understand that God works in the miraculous. Although He could just rapture us from this fight or raise us in the sky above our enemies to make it easier to pick them off one by one, He doesn't. Instead, He elevates our minds in the midst of the battle, with nothing more than His word. You see, the moment the Holy Ghost brings the word of God back to our remembrance it's like Braveheart finally hearing that voice on the other end of that radio.

Knowing that God cannot go back on His word gives us strength, to believe just what He says. (Numbers 23:19) Know that WHATEVER He said, no matter what it looks like is as good as done. It is this knowledge that does elevate our minds to a place where we don't even recognize what's going on around us. All we see is the fulfillment of what He said. So that even on the battle field those around you scratching their heads, much like Braveheart's men were might see. Even those wondering why you're rejoicing when you should be mourning might know. Those trying to figure out why it is that you're dancing when you ought to be running may also bare witness. The spectators that are pondering why it is you're smiling instead of frowning will soon understand. Those listening to your prayers, wondering how could you possibly be giving thanks and be full of joy, while you are still on the field in mid-battle with over half of your fellow laborers have died, will soon come to know the god you serve. They are not your enemies. They are not against you at all. They are just unaware, and searching. Although they have been trained to fight physically, and they are so understanding when it comes to believing only what they can see; what they fail to realize, is that victory is determined the moment the Lord lifts, not your body, but your mind out of whatever you are in the middle of. The moment you allow the presence of the Lord to remove those fears; The instant you accept the word of God as the more sure word of prophecy; The second you stop looking to the help around you and start looking to the God within you; at that very moment, you are victorious! Battles are fought on the grounds and the fields of soldiers, but won in the hearts and minds of men way before even the first finger is lifted. You already have victory over every obstacle that lay wait ahead of you. When you KNOW that, you'll see that.

Walk in Victory... Selah

Made in the USA
Columbia, SC
03 March 2020